Get CONNECTED to DIGITAL LITERACY

Super SOCIAL MEDIA and Awesome ONLINE SAFETY

Clive Gifford

Crabtree Publishing Company

www.crabtreebooks.com

Crabtree Publishing Company
www.crabtreebooks.com
1-800-387-7650

Published in Canada
Crabtree Publishing
616 Welland Ave.
St. Catharines, ON
L2M 5V6

Published in the United States
Crabtree Publishing
PMB 59051, 350 Fifth Ave.
59th Floor,
New York, NY

Published in 2018 by CRABTREE PUBLISHING COMPANY.

First published in 2017 by Wayland
(A division of Hachette Children's Books)
Copyright © Hodder & Stoughton 2017

Author: Clive Gifford
Project editor: Sonya Newland
Designer: Tim Mayer
Editors: Sonya Newland, Kathy Middleton
Proofreader: Petrice Custance
Prepress technician: Ken Wright
Print and production coordinator: Margaret Amy Salter

Consultant: Lee Martin, B. Ed, E-Learning Specialist

Photographs:
All images courtesy of Shutterstock except: iStock: p.20l (AnastasiaRasstrigina); Wikimedia: p.7t (LPS.1), p14 (secretlondon123)

While every attempt has been made to clear copyright, should there be any inadvertent omission this will be rectified in future editions.

Disclaimer: The website addresses (URLs) included in this book were valid at the time of going to press. However, because of the nature of the Internet, it is possible that some addresses may have changed, or sites may have changed or closed down since publication. While the author and publisher regret any inconvenience this may cause the readers, no responsibility for any such changes can be accepted by either the author or the publisher.

Note to reader: Words highlighted in bold appear in the Glossary on page 30.

Printed in the USA/072017/CG20170524

Library and Archives Canada Cataloguing in Publication

Gifford, Clive, author
    Super social media and awesome online safety / Clive Gifford.

(Get connected to digital literacy)
Includes index.
Issued in print and electronic formats.
ISBN 978-0-7787-3630-1 (hardcover).--
ISBN 978-0-7787-3634-9 (softcover).--
ISBN 978-1-4271-1959-9 (HTML)

    1. Online social networks--Juvenile literature. 2. Social media--Juvenile literature. 3. Computer networks--Juvenile literature. 4. Internet and children--Juvenile literature. 5. Online social networks--Security measures--Juvenile literature. 6. Social media--Security measures--Juvenile literature. I. Title.

TK5105.88817.G54 2017   j006.7'54083   C2017-903183-X
                                             C2017-903184-8

Library of Congress Cataloging-in-Publication Data

CIP available at the Library of Congress

Contents

4   Keeping in Touch

6   Social Media History

8   Facebook

10 Instant Messaging and Microblogging

12 Sharing Photos

14 Connecting to Social Media

16 How Information Spreads

18 The Business of Social Media

20 Signing Up and Starting Out

22 Keeping It Private

24 Smart, Safe Social Media

26 Social Media Issues

28 Cyberbullying

30 Glossary

31 Further Resources

32 Index

Keeping in Touch

Facebook, Snapchat, Twitter, Instagram… these and many other **applications**, called apps for short, allow you to keep in touch with people using digital technology. These applications are known as social media, and they've changed the way people work, live, and communicate with others.

You can share videos easily on many social media sites.

Share and share alike

Traditional sources of information, such as books and TV, are created by a small number of people and are read or viewed by many people who usually have no communication with one another. Social media is different because many people can create and share content, and communicate with each other and with viewers. Content can be words, illustrations, photos, and videos.

It's booming!

There are many reasons why social media is so popular today. Most social media sites are free to use, and it also makes staying connected with others easy and instantaneous. Keeping in touch with messages is often as simple as a few clicks on a tablet, smartphone, or other digital device.

You can sometimes get useful information by reading content on social media sites and chatting with members of the site.

Some social media apps allow you to alter pictures, using filters or special effects. For example, you could turn your **selfie** into a doggie-you and share it with others!

People post news about themselves and their families, and share news stories over social media.

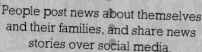

TRUE STORY

Tweets from the Top of the World

In April 2010, adventurer Eric Larsen was the first person to tweet, that is, send a message using Twitter, from the North Pole. Later that same year, he sent another tweet, this time from the top of Mount Everest, the highest mountain on Earth.

 Content kings and queens

Many types of social media help people produce their own content. This means that users do not need special computer skills to create a personal page on a social media site or share a photo with their friends.

You can comment on, "Like," or sometimes even share someone else's content with others.

Social Media History

Social media is an integral part of today's digital world, but it has only been with us a short while. People were able to connect with one another using email and electronic bulletin boards as far back as the 1980s. Social media websites took off later, in the 1990s and 2000s.

 Bulletin boards

The first elements of social media could be found on bulletin board systems (BBSs) in the late 1970s. These were simple computer noticeboards to which users sent messages and files. They often did this by connecting the computer to a telephone line to make what was often an expensive long-distance call.

 Online community

In 1995, GeoCities was launched. This web hosting service offered people the chance to create their own simple homepage on the World Wide Web. Homepages were stored on the GeoCities **server**. By the end of the 1990s, it was one of the most popular sites on the Web.

 Social media pioneers

In 1995, Classmates became one of the first social networks. The site was used by school and college friends to keep in touch. SixDegrees.com followed in 1997, and was considered by many to be the first true social media site. At its peak it had 3.5 million users, but it closed in 2001. These sites were followed in the 2000s by Friends Reunited in the United Kingdom, and Friendster, Myspace, and others in the United States.

TRUE STORY

Short-Lived Social Site
WalMart launched The Hub as a social media site for teenagers in 2006. It lasted just 10 weeks before closing down!

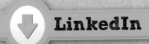

LinkedIn

LinkedIn was designed to help professional people make career connections rather than friends. The site allowed them to **upload** and share their resumes, find out about job opportunities, and link with people in similar industries. By late 2016, when Microsoft bought LinkedIn for $26.4 billion US, it had more than 450 million members.

COMPUTER Hero!

Before modern social media, people often shared images and other file types by email. American programmer Nathaniel Borenstein created the code that allowed emails to carry these files, known as attachments. Before this, emails could only include a message in text. Borenstein's first two attachments were a photo and sound file of his barbershop quartet singing!

How Much Time Do You Spend Online?

A worldwide survey* in 2016 found that individuals have an average of eight social media accounts. 32 percent of the amount of their time spent on the **Internet** was devoted to social media. People aged 16–24 averaged 2 hours and 40 minutes a day on social media.

*GlobalWebIndex quarterly report 2017

Soaring social media

Social media made a major leap forward with the arrival of smartphones and tablets. These devices could link to the Internet without wires, which allowed people to post updates and share pictures and information while they were on the move. By the end of 2016, almost a third of the people on the planet used social media.

Facebook

The biggest and most popular social network of all is Facebook. It began in 2004 as the facebook.com, at Harvard University. A student, Mark Zuckerberg, created the website with some friends as a way for students to keep in touch and learn more about each other.

Finding friends

Facebook was **innovative** because it created an online community. Members could search for people, keep in constant contact, and share information instantly with as many people as they had on their "friends" list. You could type "What's on your mind?" any time of day in your Timeline, or workspace, for your friends to read. You could read what they were writing on their accounts through your own news feed—the list of stories on your home page that is automatically updated.

Facebook expands

By the end of 2005, Facebook was booming. It had spread to more than 2,000 colleges and over 25,000 high schools across the United States. Within three years, it boasted 100 million users. By late 2016, the company claimed an incredible 1.8 billion users. That's almost a quarter of the 7.4 billion people on the entire planet!

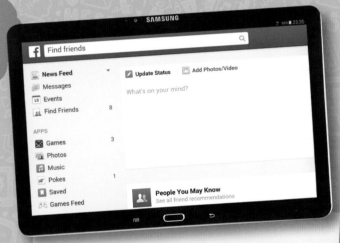

TRUE STORY

Separated at Birth In 2013, two 25-year-old Facebook friends, Anaïs Bordier who lived in France, and Samantha Futerman who lived in the United States, found out that they were twin sisters who had been born in South Korea but adopted by different families.

Facebook also introduced the idea of non-text options for commenting. For example, the "Like" button allows users to agree with another user's post, or approve of an image or video, with one click. Being able to Like other people's posts proved incredibly popular: By March 2013, an amazing 4.5 billion Likes were being produced each day!

Facebook Live

As new sites have joined social media, Facebook has continued to introduce new features to stay competitive. In 2015, Facebook Live was launched, allowing users to **stream** their own videos simply by tapping a "Go Live" button. Video created by the user's smartphone or tablet could be watched in real time by their friends on Facebook.

COMPUTER Hero!

Facebook's color scheme is blue because Mark Zuckerberg suffers from red-green color blindness.

Facebook creator Mark Zuckerberg was only 12 years old when he created his first social network. Zucknet connected members of his family. He continued **coding** as a teenager, creating Facemash, a site that allowed students to vote for the most attractive member. According to *Forbes* magazine, Zuckerberg was worth a cool $49.3 billion US in 2016!

There are now six ways of reacting to Facebook content: Like, Love, Haha, Wow, Angry, and Sad.

As of January 2017, the most Likes received worldwide by any one individual's personal page on Facebook was 118.6 million for Portuguese soccer star Cristiano Ronaldo.

Instant Messaging and Microblogging

Instant messaging (IM) and microblogging are forms of speedy social media, made up of brief messages. These allow information such as sports scores, news updates, and meeting times to be passed on quickly.

 ## Instant messaging

Instant messaging is a type of two-way chat using short text messages sent over the Internet or another computer network. The first worldwide messaging program, launched in 1996, was ICQ ("I Seek You"). Messaging programs are called clients, and Facebook Messenger, WhatsApp, Kik Messenger, and Snapchat are among the best known.

 ## Microblogging

Microblogging is simply a shorter version of a **blog**. People usually just text short messages or send a link to a website. People use microblogs to share rapid updates on their day. Friendfeed and Tumblr are popular microblogging sites, but the most famous today is Twitter.

 ## Twitter

Launched in 2006, Twitter offered users the chance to make and share short messages called tweets. Messages can contain up to 140 letters, numbers, and symbols. This might seem similar to instant messages, but tweets are public, they last forever, and can be searched by anyone, not just Twitter members.

Many celebrities use Twitter to create a more personal connection with their fans. The three most-followed people on Twitter at the start of 2017 were all pop stars: Katy Perry, Justin Bieber, and Taylor Swift.

Follower and following

If you "follow" someone on Twitter, you receive all the tweets they post. The number of people you are following, as well as the number of followers you have yourself, are displayed at the top of your **profile** page. Most of this page is devoted to the feed where new, incoming tweets are displayed.

#HASHTAGS

A hashtag (#) is a tag used on Twitter and some other social media sites. It is used directly before a word or phrase in a tweet, and the words that follow are a sort of subject label attached to the tweet. For example, if you're tweeting about your new bike, you might include, #mountainbike or #age13birthday. Hashtags make it easier for users to find messages with a specific theme or content.

STRETCH YOURSELF

Tweet Without Joining Twitter!

Try to write clear, entertaining messages in no more than 140 characters to:

☞ tell people you have a new pet,

☞ share that you got the top mark on a test,

☞ recommend that people read a particular book.

Think about how you can get your point across so everyone can understand. Come up with one, two, or three hashtag words to make each tweet easier to search for.

Sharing Photos

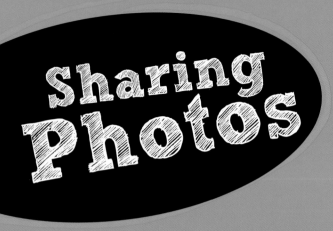

Everyone likes to take photos of the interesting things they see, their friends, or even themselves. (Selfie much?) Many popular social media sites are built specifically to let you share your photos. New social media sites need to be innovative to make them stand out from their competitors.

 ## Instagram

Instagram was one of the first sites based on photo-sharing on social media. Instantly successful, the site is used today by more than 400 million people. Instagram allows you to take photos that appear instantly on your profile to be shared with others. Fun features include filters to give your pictures different looks.

Each person's profile lists the number of people following them on Instagram.

Snapchat

Launched in 2011, Snapchat's unique feature is photos that self-destruct! Members can send a picture or short video with a caption or written message. When it is opened, the person who received it has just 10 seconds to view it before it disappears! Snapchat's over 300 million users sent an average of 9,000 images every second in 2016!

YouTube

The very first video shown on the world's most popular video-sharing site, YouTube, showed one of its three founders, Jawed Karim, visiting the San Diego Zoo. Since its launch in 2005, YouTube has grown into an enormous collection of online videos, uploaded by the public.

Pinterest

Another unique image-sharing site, Pinterest was inspired by an ordinary bulletin board. Pinterest is a site where people can gather images from websites and "pin" them to their personal pinboard for others to view. Some people use Pinterest to organize pictures about a subject they're interested in. Other Pinterest users add images they have seen on other people's pinboards to their own, using the "Re-pin" button.

COMPUTER Heroes!

Mike Krieger and Kevin Systrom founded Instagram in 2010, in California. It was launched as a mobile-phone app later that year, and gained 100,000 users in its first week. In 2012, less than two years after its launch, Facebook bought Instagram for $1 billion US!

Flickr

TRUE STORY

Top YouTuber Internet celebrity PewDiePie (whose real name is Felix Kjellberg) is the most-followed person on YouTube. His channel of YouTube videos had 52 million subscribers at the start of 2017.

Flickr is another site that took inspiration from the traditional way of presenting photos. Designed to act as a digital photo album, users of Flickr can organize large numbers of photos into groups, called galleries, and share them with others. Photo albums in digital form have the added benefit of allowing users to edit their photos or add special effects.

13

Connecting to Social Media

The key to social media's popularity is that it creates communities of people with common interests. To communicate with one another, members must first connect their device to a social media service.

Early connections

In the 1980s, computer users mostly shared files and messages by connecting their computer to a telephone line using a device called an acoustic coupler (shown below). Some of these operated at speeds thousands of times slower than today's Internet connections.

Getting online

Today, people usually connect with social media using the Internet or another computer network. An Internet connection may feature wires running from a home computer to a device called a router-modem. The modem part turns computer data into signals that can be sent through telephone lines. The router part creates a computer network, allowing different computers and devices in the home to link up.

Without wires

Many routers create a wireless area known as a **Wi-Fi** zone or hotspot. This means that devices such as smartphones, tablets, and some smart TVs can connect to the Internet without the use of wires or cables. Wi-Fi sends and receives radio signals to and from your digital devices.

Social media sites need space to handle the huge amounts of information its members create. Some sites use tens of thousands of servers. These servers are often grouped together in large centers called server farms. Twitter's server farm in Atlanta covers an area the size of 17 football fields!

Go with the Flow

User
A user is a person who can send and receive posts to social media sites. To post, the user's device connects to the Internet using a radio signal. The user's post is sent to the social media site's host.

Host
The social media site uses a series of powerful computers called servers. The servers act as the host, storing all the site's information, photos, videos, and other files sent by its users. The host also sends information out to other social media users.

Receiver 1
A user who is connected to the Internet receives the message from the host. This girl is connected through her home computer.

Receiver 2
Any user that receives the poster's message can add a comment to the post. The comment is sent back to the host through their device, and the host sends it back out to other users.

TRUE STORY

Social Media in Space
Satellites in space orbiting around Earth link people to social media. In 2010, American astronaut T.J. Creamer sent the first live tweet from space. He wrote: "Hello Twitterverse! We r now LIVE tweeting from the International Space Station."

How Information Spreads

When you join social media, you make connections with others. These people are often referred to as "friends," even if they are not friends in the traditional sense. You may not even know them in real life!

 Going viral

When you post a message on a social media site to your list of friends, some of them may share it with their list of friends. Very likely, not all of their friends will be on your friends list. Their friends may then share it with their own list, and so on. Messages and information can travel through social networks widely and rapidly this way. A post that becomes really well known and popular in a short time is described as having "gone **viral**."

 Linking social media

Many people link their social media accounts on different sites. This means what they post on their Instagram account, for example, can be seen on their accounts on other sites such as Flickr or Facebook. Accounts with the same email address can be linked so that posting an update on one will automatically post it on the others.

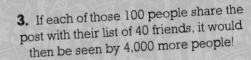

3. If each of those 100 people share the post with their list of 40 friends, it would then be seen by 4,000 more people!

2. Five of Jenny's friends, all of whom have 20 friends on their lists, comment on Jenny's post. The post and comments can now seen by 100 more people.

1. Jenny enjoys an ice cream and posts about it to her 20 friends on social media.

Popular posts or links that gather a lot of views, shares, retweets, or reposts are described as **trending**. Many social media sites feature these posts in a trending panel or box. This allows users not only to see what their own friends have posted, but also what other topics are hot with members right now.

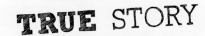

TRUE STORY

Animal lovers Animal photos, videos, and stories are popular subjects on social media. An image of a baby panda in China sneezing loudly and startling its mother went viral. By the start of 2017, it had been viewed on YouTube over 221 million times!

STRETCH YOURSELF

On the Level

Choose a famous person in history. Imagine what sort of posts, photos, and comments he or she might have made if today's social media had been available. Think of how this person might have used different types of social media to communicate different things. For example:

☞ Design a simple Facebook profile of a famous figure from history.

☞ Write some tweets from that person, as well as his or her friends, and enemies.

☞ Imagine several photographs your person might have uploaded to social media if smartphones had been invented.

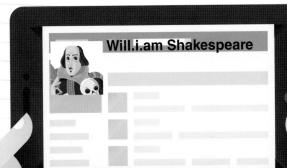

Will.i.am Shakespeare

The Business of Social Media

Nearly all social media is free, but it can cost media companies a lot of money to build and maintain their sites. So how can they afford these high costs?

Advertisers and advertising

The main way that social media companies make money is by charging other companies to advertise on their pages. Advertising is big business in the digital world. More than a third of all advertising spending in the United States in 2016 was on the Internet. In the same year, Instagram was paid over $2 billion US by advertisers.

TYPES OF ONLINE ADVERTISING

Display ads often appear at the top of a screen or in a bar running down the side of a page. Social media companies may charge advertisers by how many of their members click on these ads. Clicking takes members to the advertiser's website.

 Companies sometimes sponsor stories or posts on social media.

 Apps often contain advertising. These are sometimes called **app-verts**.

 Celebrities and experts are often paid to promote a product or service on their own social media pages.

Selling your habits

Data is information that social media sites collect about their users. Some companies, such as Twitter and Facebook, make money by selling data about their users. This is known as "data licensing." Companies collect information such as your age, location, and some of your interests, such as which celebrities, bands, or sports teams you follow. Advertisers use this information to target their products to users whose information indicates they like similar products.

Not quite free

Joining a social media site may be free, but users sometimes have to pay for certain features or additional benefits. This option is called a **freemium**. Flickr, for example, offers users a certain amount of space to upload and share their photos. To get unlimited space, users pay for the "premium" service.

TRUE STORY

Money-spinners Facebook makes some of its money from the games hosted on its site. A lot of people play these games, which include 8 Ball Pool, Pet Rescue Saga, and Clash of Clans. The top 10 games on Facebook in October 2016 were played by 340 million people during that month.

Signing Up and Starting Out

Social media sites all work in different ways and have their own rules. Most insist that you become a member before you can use their services. This means giving details about yourself. Beware! Always ask an adult before signing up for anything!

Profile page

Most social media sites expect you to complete a profile page with basic information about yourself. Be careful what you say here. To connect with people with interests similar to yours, you might mention some of your general interests, for example, cats. Don't give specific information such as your address.

Age limit

On many social media sites, including Facebook, Instagram, Pinterest, Tumblr, Reddit, and Snapchat, you must be at least 13 years old to become a member. Other sites, such as WhatsApp, set the minimum age at 16. These limits are there to protect children, in case some users try to share information that is not suitable for younger people.

Some people use a cartoon or made-up image to represent themselves on their profile page. This is called an **avatar**. It is always safer to use an avatar instead of a personal photo.

COMPUTER Hero!

A kid from California, Zach Marks, was twice removed from Facebook after he set up accounts before he was 13. Instead of sulking, Zach decided to create his own social network for kids, with his father's help. Grom Social was launched in 2012 and allows children to sign up (with a parent or guardian) to chat, share videos, play games against one another, and get help with their homework. By 2016, the site had over 3.5 million members.

Social media for tweens

Today, there are plenty of fun, safe social media sites for kids. Kidzworld is one of the most popular. Members can swap TV and movie reviews, send messages in chat rooms, and play online arcade games against each other. Other sites, such as Kuddle, allow children to share photos in a safe way. Some offer instant messaging, such as PlayKids.

STRETCH YOURSELF

Design Your Own Social Network
Grab some paper, pens, and even friends to help you design your own social network. Think about these questions:

☞ What would you call it?

☞ What features would it offer members?

☞ How would you make it easy for members to create and share content?

☞ How would it be different from existing social media?

☞ How would you make it safe and suitable for young people to use?

Keeping It Private

You may have to give information about yourself to a social media company to join their site. But that doesn't mean you have to share it with everyone on the site!

What is personal data?

Personal data is anything about you, from your address and age to the school you go to, the names of your brothers and sisters, what your parents do for a living, and where they work. You should not share this information on social media sites.

Home alone

Personal details can be misused by others. For example, burglaries have been reported because posts by users away on vacation end up revealing that their homes are empty. Also, be aware that smartphones and many tablets can pinpoint your position on the planet using GPS or other satellite navigation systems. If you leave this option on and it appears in your status updates, everyone knows when your phone—and you—are not at home!

Password power

Your password to a social media site is your first line of defense when it comes to privacy. It's something you probably rarely think about—until you forget it! If someone has your password and other details, they may be able to log in to your account and pretend to be you on a social network. Never share!

Privacy settings

Within many social media sites there are settings that allow you to decide how much or how little you share with the outside world. For example, Facebook has a range of privacy settings for photos and messages. You can choose from:

- Public: anyone can see this material including people not on Facebook.
- Friends: only your Facebook friends can view your material.
- Custom: you can pick and choose which people get to view your content.
- Only Me: for your eyes only.

If a social media site has no privacy settings, then people you don't know may be able to see all your content.

STRONG AND WEAK PASSWORDS

Passwords are ranked by their strength. A weak password is one that other people could figure out quite easily. These might include a simple sequence of letters or numbers, such as 1234567 or WXYZ, or it might be your name or the year you were born. Follow these tips to keep your data safe:

Mix numbers and upper- and lower-case letters to create a strong password.

Use a different password for your email and each social media site you use.

Never tell other members of a social media site your password.

Password

****

Forgot your password?

STRETCH YOURSELF

Create a Password

Try to come up with a bulletproof password—one that even your best friend won't be able to guess. If you're struggling, try using an online password generator such as:

https://identitysafe.norton.com/password-generator/.

This site will create a password in a flash! Use the Create Passwords section at the righthand side of the page. It allows you to choose the number of characters you want, and whether you want to include numbers and punctuation symbols.

Smart, Safe Social Media

Connecting with friends and sharing content on the Internet can be great fun—but only if you remember to be smart and thoughtful.

Be a social media star

Here are five top tips to succeed on social media.

1. Have patience. Building a network of friends online can take time. Don't worry if someone you know won't link with you. It's probably not personal. They may simply prefer to have a small number of connections, or they may use social media only occasionally.

2. Stay positive. Even if you don't agree with someone else's opinion or interests, don't be rude or make fun of them. Studies show that people who are friendly and positive often gain more followers and friends online.

3. Be interesting. Don't just post what you had for lunch–unless it was really unusual or you ate somewhere strange!

If something funny happens at school or on the weekend, take your time to write it up in an interesting or amusing way. A word of caution, though: do not give the real names or personal details of other people involved without their permission.

4. Be helpful. If you're asked questions on social media, answer them politely and quickly, as long as they're not asking for personal data. If you see someone is struggling with something and you can help, do so. Chances are you'll need help with something sometime.

5. Stay active. Posting and updating regularly is more likely to attract friends or followers. That doesn't mean you should be obsessed with going online every day. Stay active in all parts of your life. Get away from social media sometimes and actually spend time with friends in person, too!

A comment on commenting

Acting in a polite, friendly way on social media will gain you respect and avoid problems. Here are some dos and don'ts:

- **Do** consider how the things you say might affect others. Do people really want or need to know what you're about to share?
- **Don't** type things or share images that other people might find offensive.
- **Do** ask permission before posting or sharing pictures or details of someone.

- **Don't** get upset or angry and post something you may regret later. If you feel yourself turning red, take a break from your computer, smartphone, or tablet and go do something else that you enjoy.

TRUE STORY

There For All to See.

A 2016 survey in the United States showed that 60 percent of employers now look through a person's social media content when they apply for a job. A person's digital footprint sometimes influences whether he or she gets the job or not. A large number of colleges also review students' social media use.

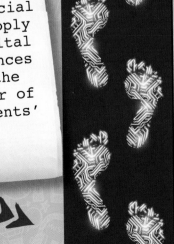

Digital footprint

Your digital footprint is all the evidence of your time online. This includes every word, photo, and video you've ever uploaded. All this material continues to exist and may be accessed by others far into the future. Remember: every time you go on social media, visit websites, or send messages in a chat room, you are increasing your digital footprint.

Social Media Issues

Social media is wildly popular and has gained a large audience. Sadly, it has also attracted people whose goal is to upset others or cause harm. Children and teenagers are often their targets.

 Not who they say they are

People with bad intentions like social media because they can hide behind a username and avatar, or pretend to be someone else. There have been instances in which adults have pretended to be children to lure younger, online "friends" to meet with them in person. This is dangerous, and it is important to remember that someone online might not be who they say they are.

 Trolls

Trolls are people who deliberately upset or disrupt others online by posting nasty comments or perhaps giving advice that backfires. Trolls find pleasure in trying to provoke arguments. Being trolled is never fun but don't respond to it. Just let a parent or teacher know.

 Griefers

Griefers are trolls in online games. They find glee in trying to spoil the play of another gamer. They might do this by stopping them from playing, or by blocking their chances of doing well in the game.

Griefers have been known to damage or destroy other players' buildings in Minecraft.

NEVER agree to meet someone in real life without a parent present, especially if you only know them on social media.

Unfriending and blocking

If someone keeps bothering you by trolling you or sending content that you don't want, you do not necessarily have to leave your favorite social media site or create a new account. Some social media sites allow you to remove the link between you and the other person.

On Facebook, you can unfriend someone so that they are no longer part of your **network**. You can also block them. This stops both of you from seeing each other's comments. It means the other person cannot add you as a friend or invite you to events. If you later sort out your issues, you can unblock them.

Feeling uncomfortable

If you receive something that upsets you or makes you feel uncomfortable, such as violent videos, sexual images, or disturbing stories and messages, stop looking or reading. Leave your computer or device and talk to a parent, a teacher, or another adult you trust. Get the adult to report the problem to the site.

STRETCH YOURSELF

Collecting Evidence

One of the most important things you can do if you are trolled, or sent rude or inappropriate messages or images, is to collect and store all the material as evidence. If you don't have a printer, you can take a **screenshot**:

Apple iPhone and iPad: Press and hold the Sleep/Wake button on the top or side, then press and release the Home button. The screenshot will appear in the Camera Roll of the Photos app.

Android: Many Android phones and tablets allow you to take a screenshot by pressing the Power button and either the Volume Down or the Home button at the same time.

Windows 8 and 10: Pressing both the Windows and Print Screen keys at the same time will capture the entire screen.

Windows 7: Use the Snipping tool found in All Programs when you press the Windows Start button, usually found in the bottom left corner of the screen. This will call up a rectangle that can be enlarged to full screen by dragging on the corner with the mouse.

Cyber-bullying

Cyberbullying is the use of technology to **harass**, threaten, or embarrass another person, usually a child or teenager. The cyberbully may repeatedly use text messages, instant messaging, emails, and social media.

What is cyberbullying?

According to a 2015 survey, almost one in six of all American schoolchildren reported they were victims of cyberbullying. What sorts of things happened to them?

- The bully constantly sent rude or disturbing messages or images.

- The bully wrote things about the victim that were untrue and shared them with other people on social media.

- The bully posted online rude or embarrassing jokes or pictures about the victim.

- The bully shared with everyone personal information or secrets they had been told by the victim in the past.

- The bully threatened the victim, saying that they were going to confront or hurt them.

Tackling cyberbullies

There are a number of things you can do to combat cyberbullying:

- Don't blame yourself. It is the cyber-bully who has a problem, not you.

- Tell an adult you trust, such as a parent, teacher, or caregiver.

- Don't reply to the bully or try to pay them back by sending similar messages and posts about them. This will only make things worse and may lead you to become a cyberbully too.

- Keep all the bullying posts, messages, and images. Store all the evidence of bullying by saving, printing, or making screenshots (see page 27) of them.

- Block the bully from any social media accounts you use (see page 27).

The accidental cyberbully

It is possible to become part of a cyberbullying problem without realizing it. To Like or Share messages or images that could be hurtful or embarrassing to others can make someone feel like everyone is against them. Always ask yourself how you would feel if it happened to you. If you think you may have upset someone in this way, apologize to them. You'll both feel better!

TRUE STORY

Paying the Price.
Cyberbullying is a crime in many countries. Teenagers have been charged with cyberbullying in the United States, and convicted and jailed in Canada and the United Kingdom. Being under 18 years of age is no defense against a charge of cyberbullying.

STRETCH YOURSELF

Tackling Cyberbullying

Get a better understanding of how cyberbullying occurs and how to avoid becoming a bully yourself at the address below.

 www.digizen.org/resources/digizen-game.aspx

At the Digizen website, you can take on a character, and role-play an entire day at school. The activity shows how cyberbullying can occur, and that people have a choice to either ignore cyberbullying or tackle it.

Glossary

applications (apps for short) Software programs downloaded and run on a smartphone or tablet

app-verts Advertising designed to be placed in apps and computer games

avatar An image used to represent a person online that is not a photo of them

blog Short for web log , a list of diary or journal entries posted on a web page for others to read

browser A type of program used to view websites on the World Wide Web

coding Writing the lines of code, or instructions, in a program that make a computer or devices work

cyberbullying The use of digital technology, such as text messages, social media, and instant messaging, to harass, threaten, or bully someone

freemium A pricing technique, where the user gets the basic version of a site or application free of charge, but must pay for additional features

griefer Someone who deliberately tries to ruin an online game for other users

harass To irritate or torment someone repeatedly

innovative Describing something or someone that uses ideas or methods in new ways

Instant messaging (IM) A type of direct communication using text between two or more people

Internet A network that connects millions of computers all over the world

network Two or more computers or digital devices linked together in some way so that they can communicate with one another

profile The collection of photos, stories, and text about your personal interests that you include on a social media site

satellites Machines traveling in space around Earth that perform useful work, such as sending TV or Internet signals to different parts of the planet

screenshot A picture of something that appears on-screen on a computer or digital device

selfie A photograph that you take of yourself using your cell phone

server A computer system in a network that sends information to a number of computers on the network

stream To send a constant flow of data over a computer network to play music or show a video

trending A topic, such as a news story or funny image, that is one of the most talked about on a social media network at the time

troll Someone who deliberately sends upsetting or annoying messages on social media to disrupt a group or start arguments

upload To send a computer file from one computer to another or, if connected to a network, sending the file to the network for others to view, use, and share

viral Quickly and widely spread or made popular from person to person

Wi-Fi Wireless local area network technology that allows people to connect computers and other digital devices to one another and to the Internet

Further Resources

Books

Privacy and Digital Security (Media Literacy) by Megan Fromm (Rosen, 2015)

Social Networking and Social Media Safety (Stay Safe Online) by Eric Minton (Powerkids Press, 2014)

Websites

www.girlshealth.gov/safety/internet/blogging.html
A great site for tips on staying safe online when using social networks.

http://bit.ly/2rUbdrX
This awesome interactive activity from the US Federal Trade Commission lets you practice setting up a fictional profile page on social media for a character named Emily.

http://www.netsmartzkids.org
Music, videos, and games offer great advice on how to stay safe online when using social media.

Index

A
acoustic coupler 14
advertising 18, 19
age restrictions 20, 21
animals 17
app 4, 5, 10, 13, 18, 20, 27
app-verts 18
attachments 7
avatar 20, 26

B
Bieber, Justin 10
blocking 27
blog 10
Bordier, Anaïs 8
Borenstein, Nathaniel 7
bulletin board 6

C
celebrities 10, 18, 19
chat room 21, 25
children 7, 20, 21, 26
Clash of Clans 19
Classmates 6
code 7
coding 9
companies 18, 19
computer 6, 10, 14, 15, 25, 27
content 4, 5, 23, 24, 27
Creamer, T. J. 15
cyberbullying 28–29

D
data licensing 19
digital footprint 25
Digizen 29

E
8 Ball Pool 19
email 6, 7, 23, 28

F
Facebook 4, 8–9, 13, 16, 17, 19, 20,
    21, 23, 27, 29
Facebook Live 9
Facebook Messenger 10
Facemash 9
filters 5, 12
Flickr 13, 16, 19
followers 11, 13, 24
freemium 19
Friendfeed 10
friends 16, 23, 24, 26, 27
Friends Reunited 6
Friendster 6
Futerman, Samantha 8

G
games 19, 21, 26
GeoCities 6
GPS 22
griefers 26
Grom Social 21

H
Harvard University 8
hashtag 11
homepage 6
host 15
Houghton, Keeley 29
Hub, The 6

I
ICQ 10
Instagram 4, 12, 13, 16, 18, 20
instant messaging (IM) 10, 21, 28
Internet 7, 10, 13, 14, 15, 18, 24

K
Karim, Jawed 12
Kik Messenger 10
Krieger, Mike 13
Kuddle 21

L
Larsen, Eric 5
Like 5, 9, 29
LinkedIn 7
links 7, 10, 14, 15, 16, 17, 24, 27

M
Marks, Zach 21
microblogging 10
Microsoft 7
modem 14
Mount Everest 5
Myspace 6

N
news 4, 5, 10, 14
news feed 8
North Pole 5

P
password 22, 23
Perry, Katy 10
personal data 22, 24
personal page 5, 9
Pet Rescue Saga 19
PewDiePie 13
photos 4, 5, 7, 12–13, 15, 17, 19, 20,
    21, 23, 25
Pinterest 13, 20
PlayKids Talk 21
posts 7, 9, 15, 16, 17, 18, 22, 24, 25,
    28
privacy 22–23
profile 11, 12, 17, 20

R
radio signal 14, 15
Reddit 20
Ronaldo, Cristiano 9
router 14
rules 20

S
satellites 15, 22
screenshot 27, 28
selfie 5, 12
server 6, 15
SixDegrees.com 6
smartphone 4, 7, 9, 14, 15, 17, 22, 25
Smart TV 14
Snapchat 4, 10, 12, 20
sound file 7, 14
Swift, Taylor 10
Systrom, Kevin 13

T
tablet 4, 7, 9, 14, 22, 25, 27
teenagers 6, 9, 26, 28
telephone line 14
trending 17
trolls 26, 27
Tumblr 10, 20
Twitter 4, 5, 10, 11, 15, 19

U
unfriending 27
username 26

V
videos 4, 9, 15, 21, 25

W
WalMart 6
WhatsApp 10, 20
Wi-Fi 14
World Wide Web 6

Y
Yahoo 13
YouTube 12, 13, 17

Z
Zuckerberg, Mark 8, 9
Zucknet 9